Complete Hamster Care

Contents

Your Feedback is Important

We hope that you enjoy reading this guide. If you do, please leave a review and 5-star rating on the online bookstore where you purchased it.

If not, please get in touch and tell us what we got wrong. We welcome customer feedback on errors, omissions, typos, ideas for new books and offers of collaboration and publishing opportunities. You can email us at southcrater@virginmedia.com

Welcome to Your New Hamster

Congratulations if you have bought, or are thinking about buying a hamster, you are obviously serious about giving them the best care as you have bought this guide.

If you have adopted a rescue hamster then we think you are a superhero.

Maybe you are not sure yet if a hamster is the right pet for you. That's OK too. In the pages of this care guide, you will learn more about the time and commitment required. We will also cover the equipment needed so that you can gauge the full cost of owning a hammy.

Stewardship of any animal is a massive responsibility, regardless of its size. Your hamster will be relying on you for water, food, warmth, shelter, attention, and enrichment.

In return, you will be rewarded by spending quality time with a cute, cuddly, playful, often cheeky friend.

Over the course of the next few chapters, we will consider:

- Fun Hamster facts
- Why Hamsters make great pets
- Different breeds of hamster
- Selecting a hamster in the store
- Reasons not to own a hamster
- What your hamster needs
- Foods to avoid
- Taking care of your hamster
- Common illnesses that affect hamsters
- Training your hamster not to bite
- Determine your hamster's sex

Young or old, a hamster can enrich your life and become your best friend, your confidant and a loved member of the family.

We will also throw in a few pictures of cute hamsters, just because we love them and are sure you will too.

Fun Hamster Facts

Did you know:

- There are 24 species of hamster
- Hamsters belong to the family Cricetidae (the second largest family of mammals)
- Hamsters are related to moles, lemmings and muskrats
- The most popular breeds to keep as a pet are Syrian, Russian Dwarf Campbell and Roborovski (or Robo)
- Hamsters use their whiskers to help them sense objects in their environment
- Your hamster's teeth never stop growing
- Hamsters' teeth are self-sharpening. The incisors grind against each other while gnawing, which sharpens them and wears the teeth down
- Hamsters are generally nocturnal
- Hamsters' eyes are dominated by rods - the part of the eye that can function in lower light – which means they have better night vision
- Not all hamsters are sociable - in the wild, Syrian hamster adults generally live on their own in their burrows
- Hamsters Love to hoard food. They have cheek pouches, called displostomes, that they fill to move food around their enclosure
- Hamsters like to sleep in enclosed spaces
- Burrowing is one of the favourite activities. They use their front and back paws like you and I use our hands
- Hamsters like lots of exercise as they have a high metabolism
- Hamsters might have moods just like you and I do. A 2015 study identified that hamsters may have moods, something that many hamster owners had suspected for years

Why Hamsters make great pets

Hamsters are cute, what more do you need to know? Seriously though, here are some of the reasons why hamsters make great pets:

1. Affordable. They are relatively inexpensive

We don't just mean they are cheap compared to exotic animals like tigers or a giraffe. As far as domestic pets go, a hamster is one of the most affordable.

The initial set-up costs can be a big initial outlay but after that bedding and food is quite inexpensive. That said, don't pinch pennies. Proper bedding is essential. Other books might recommend scrunched up newspaper but often the ink contains toxins that can make your hamster very ill.

You should also budget for the inevitable vet visits that will be required. Small pet insurance is available but check that it covers everything that your hamster may suffer from and covers the whole of their life.

2.   Require Minimal Space

Unlike cats or dogs and other animals that need space to roam, your hamster can be kept in a smallish (see minimum size in the section What Your Hamster Needs) cage. A right-sized wheel will also provide them plenty of exercise.

The mess created by a hamster is, mostly, constrained to their cage. You can keep a hamster even if you live in a small apartment or shared space.

Of course, they like to roam free in your living space too if you feel brave enough.

3. Easy to Care For

Hamsters are quite easy to look after. How easy, I hear you ask - as easy as goldfish? Well probably, yes. You only really need to make sure that they are fed, have fresh water, access to a wheel for exercise and are kept clean and checked for signs of becoming unwell.

Of course, the reason for keeping a hamster is that you want to care for it, pick it up, play with it and become its best friend. But hamsters are in general solitary animals and can cope with long periods of inattention.

Just bear in mind that the less they are handed, the less sociable they will become towards you. Don't expect a cuddle without a nip from a hamster that is not used to being handled regularly.

4. Don't Require Extensive Training

Unlike a dog, your hamster doesn't need to be trained to sit, beg, rollover or not to bite the postman. You might choose to teach one or two tricks a part of your regular handling routine or for enrichment, but it's ok if you don't.

5. Low Commitment

I own a tortoise. Well, I should really say that my daughter owns a tortoise, it was just me that handed over well-earned cash to the pet store. In all honesty the tortoise will likely outlive me as they have a lifespan of 50 – 100 years.

Your hamster is more likely to have a life-span of between 2 to 3 years, maybe up to 4. That can be a real deciding actor when buying a pet for a child. Your hamster can be loved and live a full and rich life, passing away of natural causes before your youngster is bored of it.

Of course, that short life span also means that you will need to prepare for the inevitable demise of your cherished pet. Whilst that is listed later as a downside of hamster ownership, it raises the opportunity to talk about mortality, feelings and faith.

6. Great Starter Pet

As they are low maintenance, inexpensive, take up little room and are easy to care for with little long-term commitment, hamsters are considered to be great starter pets.

That is not to say that they are recommend for children. Children under 10 should always be supervised when caring for a hamster but a hamster is a good starter pet to teach a child how to care for an animal.

7. Are Good for Your Health

Owning a pet, including a hamster, can have great health benefits. Studies have shown that a pet can help to reduce blood pressure and anxiety, reduce loneliness and improve your sleep.

That last one – improve your sleep - will only hold true if your hamster doesn't have a squeaky wheel in your bedroom of course.

8. They are just so cute

You already knew that though, right? Not only are they small, fluffy and cute … they never grow up. Well, ok they get a bit bigger but they stay small, fluffy and cute for their whole life unlike a puppy or a kitten.

Just in case you needed reminding, here are more cute hamster pictures.

Different Breeds of Hamster

Attribute	Value
Name	Hamster (Crcetinae)
Class	Mammalia
Order	Rodentia
Suborder	Sciurognathi
Number of genera, species	7 genera; 18 species
Habitat	Deserts, dry plains, steppes, and cultivated fields
Distribution	Throughout the Palearctic zone of Europe and Asia

That's the science part out of the way. The exact number of hamster breeds is still somewhat disputed as being somewhere between 18 to 25. Whatever number you choose, most are not kept as pets.

The common 5 breeds popular as pets are

- Golden Hamster or Syrian (Mesocricetus Auratus)
- Campbell's Dwarf Hamster (Phodopus Campbell)
- Russian Dwarf (Phodopus Sungorus)
- Roborovski Hamster (Phodopus Roborovski)
- Chinese Hamster (Cricetulus Griseus)

There are a few things to consider when choosing the right breed of hamster for you. Breed traits include how much maintenance they require, whether or not they are sociable, if they can be kept in a group of more than one pet hamster, life expectancy, and their overall behaviours.

To help you decide which hamster breed is right for you, we will look at each one and list their common traits.

Golden Hamster / Syrian Hamster

Origins

The Golden Hamster is popularly known as the Syrian hamster due to being found in the wild in a only in a small area restricted to a region around the town of Halab, in north-western Syria where they inhabit rocky, shrubby, and dry slopes or plains.

A group of these hamsters was transported to Palestine from Syria in the 1930s and their descendants were sent all over the world to be kept as pets. Another group was captured in Syria in 1971 and taken to the US. All of the Golden Hamsters kept as petted can be traced back to one of these two groups.

Golden or Syrian Hamsters are considered to be Endangered in the wild, due mostly to loss of habitat. They are, however, thriving in captivity and are one of the most popular breeds of pets.

Characteristics

Syrian Hamsters grow to between 5 – 7 inches long and weigh 85-150g. A Syrian will usually live for around 3 years.

They are called Golden Hamsters due to their colouring, however after decades of breeding in captivity there are many different variations in colouring and not all retain the golden-brown fur on their back.

Natural colour variations include

- Golden
- Black
- Cream
- Cinnamon
- White
- Rust
- Dark Grey
- Light Grey
- Silver Grey

Breeders have created a long hair version of the golden hamster that is referred to as the Teddy Bear hamster.

Female Syrians become fertile every four days and have a short gestation period of only 16 days. Hence, we never recommend keeping a male and female together.

Syrians are very territorial and are best keep in solitary cages. Males will fight and females have been known to attack males after mating. That might surprise you as in many pet stores you will see groups of hamsters kept together in a single cage and seeming to get along. Remember that pet store hamsters are usually juveniles and their natural behaviours will become more noticeable as they grow older. A Syrian hamster kept alone will generally be docile and have an inquisitive nature.

Campbells Dwarf Hamster

Origins

Campbell's dwarf hamster was first discovered, unsurprisingly, by Charles William Campbell in Mongolia in 1902. Campbell's Dwarf hamsters are native to China, Mongolia, Kazakhstan and Russia.

The wild population is thriving and they are able to interact with human habitat, often found keeping warm inside yurts in the winter.

Characteristics

In the wild, these hamsters grow up to 3 inches long. They tend to be a little bigger when kept as pets and fed on commercial hamster food.

They tend to be grey or brown and most will show a dark, narrow dorsal stripe that runs from the neck to the centre of the back.

In captivity the Campbell Dwarf hamster will live between 2 – 2.5 years.

Like most hamsters, Campbells are nocturnal and do not like bright lights or loud noises. When awake they love to dig and burrow.

Campbells are a little less docile than the Syrian hamster and are one of the faster breeds making them more difficult to handle, especially for younger owners.

They are affectionate pets but do need regular handling or might become more prone to nipping.

Campbells are specifically more prone to diabetes and you should select a food that is specifically designed for the breed.

Whilst still prone to becoming territorial, you may have more chance of having two Campbells share a cage, make sure there is plenty of space for the two of them. From time-to-time same sex pairs will fall out and you should watch for signs of bullying or fighting. Mixed sex pairs can be kept but hamsters become sexually mature at a very young age.

Russian Dwarf Hamster / Winter White

Origins

The Russian Dwarf hamster, also known as the Winter White Dwarf or the Siberian hamster, hails from Siberia and Kazakhstan. In the wild, they are usually found in the wheat fields of Kazakhstan, the meadows of Mongolia and Siberia, and the birch stands of Manchuria.

The name Winter White comes from the fact that in the wild these hamsters change their fur colour from dark to white for the winter months. This white fur camouflages the hamster and reduces the chances of predation when the ground is covered with snow. Kept as pets it is rare for this full colour change to occur, although you may see their colour whiten.

These hamsters often are confused with Campbell's Dwarf Hamsters (also from Russia), which have a similar size and appearance.

Characteristics

Russian Dwarf Hamsters are shaped like little balls and are on average about half the size of their larger cousin the Syrian hamster.

They tend to be more ash-grey in colour and live for up to 3 years. They are one of the more vocal breeds and can be heard to squeak more than others.

They are also a bit more docile than other dwarf breeds and less prone to biting.

Roborovski Hamster

Origins

Roborovski hamster or the Robo hamster is found in the desert regions of Kazakhstan, Mongolia and Xinjiang in China. They live in areas of loose sand with little vegetation.

Continental Europe began breeding Robos in the 1990s and all of the pets found un the US and UK markets are descended from batches imported from the Netherlands between 1990 and 1998.

Characteristics

Robos are smaller than the two dwarf species and usually grow no more than 2 inches long. Naturally shy they need to be handled from a young age to make them accustomed to you as their owner.

They are also more active than all of the other hamster breeds, making them the most difficult to keep as a pet. They are said to run as much as 6 miles or 9.5 kilometres a night. That said, they can be kept as a same sex pair or small group if introduced at a young age.

The Roborovski hamster is distinguished from the Campbell's dwarf by its smaller size, sandy coloured fur and lack of a dorsal stripe. The most common colour is the agouti — a natural sandy-brown with white underside and white patches over their eyes.

Claims of Robo hamsters being hypo-allergenic are very much disputed.

Robo Hamsters are Crepuscula. That means that's whilst they do spend some time awake at night, they're most active in the morning and evening times around dawn and dusk.

Chinese Hamster
Origins

You will not be surprised to learn that the Chinese Hamster originated in the deserts of northern China and Mongolia. Chinese hamsters were first bred as lab animals and, thankfully, haven fallen out of use in the lab were kept as pets.

They are sometimes referred to as a Chinese Dwarf hamster but they are not technically as not in the same genus as the Campbell's Dwarf or Robo.

Characteristics

Their wild colour is greyish brown above with a black stripe down the spine and a whitish belly. This colour, their nimble build and longer tail, makes them look like a mouse than other breeds.

Chinese hamsters have quiet temperaments and are easily handled. One of their endearing traits is that of clinging to a finger with all four paws, rather like a harvest mouse on a corn stalk.

Chinese hamsters can be quite nervous as youngsters, however, once they are tame, display an endearing calmness and gentleness of character.

Females are generally kept as pets, and males used solely for breeding. Being naturally solitary, they can be aggressive if kept in a cage which is too small, and should be kept alone.

They can be nippy, are quickly tamed and are then easily handled.

Selecting a Hamster in the Store

Many pet stores sell hamsters, with the additional bonus that you can buy all of the equipment you need in one place. Just be aware that some stores are better than others and some might try to sell products and enclosures that are not suited to your hamster. Read this guide cover to cover before you buy.

Alternatively look online for details of local breeders, or to be a real hammy hero adopt a rescue hamster and they will love you forever.

Here are a few things to look out for when choosing your new pet:

Eyes - bright with no sign at all of cloudiness or any discharge. Dull eyes could be the sign of a serious problem.

Ears - clean with no wax build-up.

Mouth – no signs of dribbling or scabbing at the corners (signs of fighting infection or poor teeth).

Nose – clean nostrils with no mucus visible and no signs of any breathing difficulties

Fur – should have a gloss shine and have no bald patches or signs of scratching. Check for matted hair around the rump that's could be a sign of wet tail or diarrhoea. A dak patch visible on each hip is nothing to worry about, some hamsters have visible scent glands here.

Most pet stores will supply a cardboard box to bring your hamster home in. These are only suitable for very short journeys. If you live a longer distance from the store ensure that your new pet is double boxed as they might chew out of the first layer.

Think about investing in a suitable small animal carrier. You are likely to need it for vet visits and as holding pen for short periods when you are cage cleaning for example.

Baby hamster are generally weaned at three to four weeks and ready to go to a new home at about six weeks. Check with the store when your new hamster was born.

Hamsters are easier to tame when they are young. If you adopt an older hamster you will need to be extra patient but you will be a hammy hero.

Reasons Not to Own a Hamster

We love hamsters, you love hamsters but for balance we have included a short section on the reasons not to own a hamster.

1. Hamsters Bite

There, we have said it and it is true. No matter how experienced a handler you are almost everyone that owns a hamster will get bitten from time to time, especially when teaching a juvenile to be handled.

The reason hamsters bite is that they have quite poor eyesight and so investigate strange new things, like a finger pushed into a cage, by smell and taste.

Hamsters will also bite if they feel threatened, scared or surprised. A hamster that is handled regularly is less likely to bite as it will become accustomed to being picked up and not feel threatened, scared or surprised.

2. Hamsters are Nocturnal

OK so some are active around dawn and disk but most hamsters will curl up and sleep during the day. They won't take kindly to be woken either – see above. That means that they are not a pet that a child can play with when they get home from school.

Conversely, your hamster is likely to be awake and active during the night. Don't keep a hamster cage in your bedroom unless you like to sleep with the scratchy sound of burrowing or the squeak of a running wheel.

3. Hamsters Smell

This is a common assertion that we hear fairly regularly from people that don't keep hamsters. A well looked after hamster in a cage that is appropriately cleaned will smell less than most pet rodents. Hamsters are always grooming and will keep themselves clean.

However, they do have scent glands and can emit a scent that is managed by cage cleaning. Females will also have a stronger smell when they are in heat (every 4 days or thereabouts).

Any pet owner has to manage a small amount of odour. Wet dog, a cat with fishy breath and so on. Hamsters are generally not a smelly pet but if you are very sensitive to odours then, yes, they are noticeable.

4. Short Life Span

Hang on didn't we list that as a reason to own a hamster? Well yes, we did, but you do need to realize that a 3 – 4 year-old hamster is likely to pass away. The death of a pet can cause sadness, anxiety and stress.

You should also be prepared with what to do with your hamster after it has passed, will you bury it in the garden or pay for a pet cremation and how will you explain the loss to young children.

5. Adult Supervision is Required

Again, this one is probably true of all pets. But with some animals, like a dog or a cat you can expect a child to play and have fun without having to worry about the animal being harmed.

Hamsters are small and fragile and can be broken quite easily. Young children need to be taught to take great care.

Don't forget that Hamsters are sensitive to mishandling and will bite if they are mistreated (see 1). Children also need guidance on appropriate feeding, cleaning and making sure that the hamster gets enough exercise and play.

6. Illness

Hamsters can be especially susceptible to certain illnesses like diabetes, abscesses and wet tail. You will need to keep an eye open for signs of illness and be prepared to seek appropriate veterinary assistance.

It is extremely rare that hamsters pass on any illness to humans but if you keeping your hamster as a pet for a young child you should teach them proper handwashing and hygiene after handling the hamster to avoid issues with bacteria, in particular Salmonella which can cause stomach cramps, diarrhoea, and fever.

7. Responsibility

Owning a hamster is hugely rewarding but it does come with responsibility. You are responsible for the health and wellbeing of this small furry animal and will have to undertake chores like cleaning and feeding to maintain its health.

What will you do when you want to go on holiday, who will feed and look after your hamster? Do you have the time for vet visits when they are needed?

What your Hamster Needs

A hamster is a relatively inexpensive pet to keep but there can be an initial outlay to make sur that you have everything that your hamster needs. Here is a typical shopping list for a new hamster.

- ❖ Large hamster cage or enclosure
- ❖ Hamster shelter (bed)
- ❖ Burrowing and nesting material
- ❖ Hamster food
- ❖ Food dish
- ❖ Water bottle
- ❖ Cleaning Products (animal safe disinfectant)
- ❖ Exercise wheel
- ❖ Tubes and toys for enrichment
- ❖ Gnawing blocks or sticks
- ❖ Hamster treats
- ✓ Book on hamsters

Well done, as you are reading this you already have at least one thing from the list. Let's have a closer look at some of the items that you will need.

Cage or Enclosure

Size

When it comes to your hamster's enclosure bigger is better. The Animal Humane Society of the United States recommend a minimum enclosure size equivalent to a 15-gallon tank. In the UK the RSPCA used to recommend a floor area no smaller than 3,000cm^2.

Enthusiasts would recommend even bigger 4,000cm^2 for a dwarf breed and 5,000cm^2 or more for a Syrian.

When buying an enclosure be sure to check with the store that it meets the relevant requirement and check the website of these two fantastic organisations for updated advice.

Why is cage size so important? Well, to answer that question, you should firstly consider that your cute furry hamster is essentially a wild animal. They are not domesticated like cats that were kept by the ancient Egyptians or dogs that have been kept for tens of thousands of years.

In the wild a hamster might roam a territory that is over a mile square.

Hamsters that are kept in an in enclosure that is too small can exhibit some bad behaviours such as bar biting and aggression. Some owners tell me that their hamsters are just plain mean, always biting. In almost every case that meanness is no more than cage aggression from being housed in a cage that is far too small.

Similarly, bar biting is not normal, not healthy, and not safe for your hamster. It is not the same as normal gnawing behaviour. Bar biting is a frenzied act brought on by psychological stress of a cage that is too small.

Having several layers does not make up for a lack of floor space.

Material

Your hamster cage can be made from wire or glass.

When buying a wire cage, it can be tempting to choose a cage that is sold for a rabbit due to the larger footprint (see above) and lower price. Just make sure that the gaps between the wire are appropriate for a hamster, else your furry escapologist won't be in there for long.

 Alternatively, you can cover the bars with plexiglass or smaller wire mesh.

It might surprise you to learn that your hamster can live in a glass tank or a terrarium. Whilst unsuitable for many small animals like guinea pigs or rats, hamsters produce less urine and therefore less ammonia meaning that they cope well with the reduced ventilation of a glass tank. Whilst more expensive, a glass tank can be easier to clean and allows for a deeper bedding and burrowing substrate to be used.

Remember to add a mesh lid (the lid must not be solid as some ventilation is still required).

Location

Having selected a cage of the right size and material, you need to think about where your enclosure will be kept. There are a few simple rules that you will need to follow.

Hamsters don't like extreme temperature so avoid putting them in direct sunlight or near draughts and radiators. In very cold weather, you can give your hamster more bedding or move their enclosure somewhere warmer.

Hamsters are also very sensitive to high frequency sounds or ultrasound which we cannot hear. Keep your hamster away from anything that can generate ultrasound, such as TVs, computer screens, vacuum cleaners or sources of running water.

Hamsters also like routine and if you are going to regularly handle them the cage needs to be accessible. Try to put them in a room that meets the criteria above but is used regularly as well with periods of light and dark that do not vary wildly.

Shelter

Your hamster needs a nesting box or shelter to retreat to keep warm, feel safe and sleep in. It should be big enough for them to move around in too.

There are many options available in your pet store or you can use of everyday cardboard items, such as empty boxes. Your hamster will enjoy using them and chewing them when they are done. When reusing household boxes just make sure that they are not heavily printed as some inks contain toxins that will be harmful to your hamster.

Similarly ensure that you use hamster safe glue if making your own shelter. Pick a non-toxic adhesive like PVA or school glue.

Burrowing and nesting material

Your hamster will spend all of their life walking, eating, and sleeping amongst the substrate that you use to fill the cage, so choosing the right one will really improve their comfort and quality of life.

Dusty materials can cause breathing problems and must be avoided.

Chemically treated bedding can also cause health issues.

Always choose a bedding that is marked as 'dust-free' or 'dust extracted' and untreated and remember that deodorising chemicals on fragranced products aren't suitable.

Sawdust is very commonly used in small pet cages and we are often asked if it is suitable for hamsters. Unfortunately, it isn't. It can irritate your hamster's lungs as it is usually very dusty and has sharp edges that cause issue when pouched.

Fluffy bedding might look cute but it should also be avoided. Fibres can get lodged in the throat and cheek pouches leading to choking, suffocation or starvation through inability to swallow. If you hammy does eat fluffy bedding the fibres cannot be digested and intestinal blockages may occur. Finally, fluffy fibres can get trapped around toes or limbs leading to amputation.

Compressed paper bedding is a better choice as it's softer, less dusty and absorbs urine well. Teabag bedding is another popular option.

Hamsters need quite a deep layer of bedding to burrow in. The deeper the better and 5" - 6" is a good starting point.

Hamster Food and Food Dish

Most owners will feed their hamster from a ceramic bowl. Ceramic is durable, washable and is heavy enough the it can't be easily tipped.

Dwarfs look especially cute when they sit in the middle of their food bowl.

Probably the easiest and safest approach to feeding your hamster is to go with a complete hamster feed that you can find in your pet store.

There are several types that comes in square blocks or are a pelleted feed. These pellet feeds are better than a seed mixture because many hamsters will pick out only the seeds that they like from these mixes, missing out on additional nutritional value.

Feed your hamster about a tablespoon of food once a day, or enough to fill both cheek pouches. Giving your hamster any more food than that may lead them to hoarding their food. Hoarding is natural behaviour and not a huge issue unless you are feeding natural food like fruit and vegetable that will spoil and smell if left.

In addition to pellet food, your hamster can also eat:

- Broccoli
- Cauliflower
- Kale
- Cucumbers
- Celery
- Bok choy
- Sweet potatoes (No skin)
- Apples
- Cherries
- Strawberries
- Raspberries
- Peaches
- Mango
- Cantaloupe

Your hamster can also eat nuts and watching a hamster with an unopened walnut is a joy to behold, but nuts are dense in calorific and fat content so should be only an occasional treat.

Water bottle

Your hamster is vulnerable to dehydration and will not survive for more than a day or two without water. You should make sure that water is easily accessible and changed every day.

Most owners will use a vacuum-action inverted water bottle that releases water only when your hamster actively drinks from it. These attach to the outside of the metal cage

You can place water in a bowl inside the cage if preferred and some enthusiasts recommend having both a bottle and a bowl.

Hamsters also take hydration from food sources like cucumber. If you are worried that your hamster isn't drinking you must consult a veterinarian straight away.

Exercise wheel

Hamsters need an exercise wheel to get enough exercise and to mimic their natural behaviour. When buying a wheel there are a few things to consider, the most important is size.

28cm is the minimum sized wheel for a Syrian, 21cm for smaller breeds. Often cages which are too small can't fit an adequately sized hamster wheel. A small wheel can cause permanent injury to your hamster's back, leaving your hamster in unnecessary pain and discomfort.

The wheel should have a solid track and not be meshed or barred or have any kind of opening in which toes or a foot could get trapped.

Finally, for your sanity you might want to choose a 'silent' version.

Enrichment

Hamsters' enrichment needs stimulate them physically and mentally. For hamsters that might include varying food, smells and textures. To encourage your hamster to be active and to prevent boredom, you should give your hamster enrichments and boredom breakers.

Physical stimulation means offering physical enrichment such as new toys to explore, drag and chew, or opportunities for climbing (safely).

Food-based enrichment can include scattering food to encourage searching and foraging and activity to earn rewards such as treats.

Sensory stimulation, is about providing different scents, sounds and textures to stimulate the 5 senses, sight, smell, touch, hearing and taste.

Social stimulation and enrichment are provided by laytime and handing when you interact with your furry companion.

Gnawing Blocks and Treats

In the wild, hamsters will grind down their teeth by chewing on sticks and through eating a varied diet. In order to help your hamster keep their teeth in good condition and prevent overgrowing you should provide wooden blocks or wooden chew sticks. Mineral blocks can also be used but they are very hard and many hamsters won't use them.

Without items for your hamster to chew on, their teeth can become damaged or cause injury. Overgrown incisors can get so long that they stop your hamster from being able to close the mouth to eat. Overgrown incisors also can poke into the gums and tongue, causing cuts and bleeding.

Foods to Avoid

When it comes to feeding your hamster, its's best to start with a commercial pelleted food specifically made for hamsters.

Some foods must be avoided including:

- **Almonds**: Bitter almonds contain a small amount of cyanide, a poison that can be fatal for hamsters. All almonds are high in fat so anything more than the occasional piece of roasted almond should be avoided.
- **Celery**: The stringy part of a whole celery stick can get stuck in the mouth and throat and choke a hamster. Remove the strings and cut the celery into very small pieces for a safer snack.
- **Garlic**: Even moderate amounts garlic can cause indigestion and blood disorders
- **Kidney beans**: Uncooked kidney beans are poisonous to hamsters.
- **Lettuce**: Iceberg lettuce contains very little nutrition and can cause stomach upsets and diarrhea. Small amounts of other green leafy vegetables, such as dandelion greens, romaine lettuce and kale, are safer and more nutritious.
- **Onion**: Any plant in the onion family (chives, leeks and shallots) May result in blood damage.
- **Peanuts**: Nuts are high in fat, and any salted nuts will cause dehydration.
- **Potato and potato tops**: Are full of starch and will cause your hamster to gain weight quickly (akin to a human diet of chips)
- **Chocolate**: Chocolate contains theobromine and is toxic in large amounts.
- **Spicy or seasoned products**: May upset your hamster's intestinal tract and cause diarrhea.
- **Sugary products**: Hamsters love sugary foods like some shop bought treats like yoghurt drops and honey covered seeds and

will choose to eat these empty calories instead of their healthier foods. This is especially dangerous for Chinese hamsters as it can lead to diabetes.

- o **Pesticides**: Unwashed fruit and vegetables pose a danger to your hamster if they have been treated with pesticides. Organic are safer, particularly if you wish to feed the skins as well.
- o **Meats**: Hamsters have a difficult time digesting heavy meats. Light-colored meats such as chicken or fish can be processed much easier than red meats and its ok to feed the odd mealworm or cricket as a treat.

Taking Care of Your Hamster

To keep your hamster fit and healthy you need to attend to their needs and give them the care and attention required.

Food and Water

Your hamster must be given fresh water every day. It can be placed in a shallow dish inside of the cage or in an upside-down gravity fed water bottle. Water must be changed at least once a day.

If using a bottle ensure it is valve-less. Hamsters cannot create enough suction to drink from a standard ball/valve arrangement used for larger rodents. Check the bottle everyday for leaks and blockages.

Your hamster will also need to be fed every day. Feed enough to fill its cheek pouches and try to feed around the same time each day. Feeding at the same time avoids food anxiety that can lead to stress.

Food can be placed into a shallow bowl, directly onto the floor of the cage or scattered for enrichment. If you use a bowl, don't be alarmed if your hamster tips it all out or pouches all of the food and stashes it away in a special hammy hidey place.

Cleaning

It's very important to keep your hamster's home clean. You should have a daily, weekly and monthly maintenance routine to keep everything fresh and your hamster healthy.

Daily:

Remove any wet or soiled bedding every day. Hamsters will usually pee in one or two specific places in their habitat, so scoop out any wet bedding and replace it with fresh, dry bedding. Use a small scoop if you don't like to touch it with your hands (which should be washed afterwards in any case).

Clean your hamster's food bowls and water bottles daily. For the same reason that we wash up our own crockery, your hamster's bowls, dishes and water bottles should be kept clean to prevent bacterial build up and sickness or infection.

Weekly:

Clean bedding weekly. In addition to scooping out dirty bedding every day, plan to change out any dirty or smelly bedding in your hamster's habitat once a week. It is important to know that your hamster might find over-cleaning stressful so it is not absolutely necessary to change all of the bedding every week.

It is important to remove any food your hamster may have stored throughout the week, especially if you have been feeding perishable food like fresh fruit and vegetables.

Monthly:

Wash your hamster's entire habitat about once a month. This is important to prevent the build up of bacteria and also allows you to check the condition of the enclosure and ensure that it remains escape-proof.

You will need to put your hamster in a safe, temporary cage like a small animal carrier while you perform your deep clean.

Wash the enclosure, hideaways, accessories and hard toys with lukewarm, soapy water or an anti-bacterial cleaner that is made for small-animals. Check any cleaning fluids used to avoid harmful ammonia-based products.

Be sure to le the enclosure dry completely before adding fresh bedding back in.

Play Time

Daily play keeps your hamster happy and healthy and allows you to bond. Make sure that your hamster has lots of space to exercise and has appropriate objects to play with.

A good quality running wheel can provide extra opportunities for exercise but your hamster must always have lots of other things to play with as well.

Ensure your hamster has things to play with such as small boxes, wooden chew blocks, and tubes. The inner cores from toilet rolls make great inexpensive exploring and chewing opportunities.

Many owners like to let their hamster roam free. Free play is good for enrichment but be sure that your hamster will be safe from any hazards like falling from a stairwell or open windows etc. You might want to invest in a play pen and fill it with play things. Get in and play with your hamster.

The use of hamster balls is a bit of a contentious question. Whilst they look like great fun to give your hammy extra exercise and allow them to roam over a larger area safely, there are some drawbacks.

Anxiety is probably the biggest issue to consider. Hamsters have poor eyesight and being in such an enclosed space can cause a hamster to become stressed. Balls have holes for ventilation, not only can those holes be ineffective in allowing enough ventilation but your hamster could catch a toe or a foot and cause damage. There is also a tendency for the ball to bump against furniture or the wall as your hamster is less able to control momentum in a ball. These bumps can cause stress or impact injury.

Health Checks

You should check your hamster every day for any signs of injury or illness. If you suspect that your hamster is in any pain, or is ill or injured, you should visit a veterinarian immediately.

Take your hamster to a vet immediately if you notice any of the following signs:

- not eating or drinking
- sitting in a hunched-up position
- sunken or dull looking eyes
- disinterested at times when normally active
- drinking lots of water
- wet faeces and/or diarrhoea
- discharge from the nostrils, eyes, genitals etc.
- persistent sneezing or coughing
- difficulty walking or unsteady balance
- not using a limb
- persistent scratching
- suddenly more aggressive than usual
- firm, warm and swollen stomach

- any injuries or abnormal lumps.

It is important to regularly check your hamster's front teeth. If their teeth become overgrown, they need to be taken to the vet. If one incisor tooth is damaged, the other tooth can keep growing and eventually may stop your hamster eating.

Common illnesses that affect hamsters

Hamsters can suffer from a variety of different health problems. Here are some of the most common issues to look out for. If your hamster appears to be in pain, is having trouble breathing or is bleeding, you must take your pet to a small mammal vet as soon as possible.

Abscesses

The main symptom of an abscess is the development of a swelling on the body which can be soft or hard. The swelling is full of pus that the hamster's body has produced during its fight with the infection. Abscesses can form on any area of the body including the cheeks and be very painful for your hamster. An abscess will need draining and cleansing by a vet

Diarrhea

Diarrhea can be a common problem and usually indicates that your hamster is having trouble digesting certain foods. Watch out for diarrhea after a change in diet and hold off feeding fresh fruit and vegetables for a few days. Pay close attention to ensure that your hamster does not have Wet Tail.

Wet Tail

Wet tail is a potentially fatal condition for hamsters, and so action needs to be taken very quickly. Wet tail is a very serious case of diarrhoea. If your hamster has a wet tail-area (possibly with lots of faecal matter around it) and has a strange posture, then it's likely suffering from wet tail, a really painful condition often caused by bacteria.

Respiratory Infections

If your hamster is coughing, wheezing, sneezing, has a runny nose or eyes, or is having difficulty breathing, then it may be suffering from a respiratory infection. Respiratory infections will need vet treatment. Hamsters can catch coughs and colds just like us.

Urinary Infections

A drastic change in the colour of your hamster's urine or blood in their pee could be a sign of a urinary infection. Vet time again.

Skin Conditions

Hamsters are prone to a number of skin conditions that can be caused by mange (a very unpleasant mite that actually burrows underneath your pet's skin), mites or fleas. The most obvious sign to look for is continued scratching, especially at a single area.

Diabetes

Diabetes can occur in a number of hamster species, but it is most common among dwarf hamsters. Look for signs of excessive drinking and urinating, shaking and a low body temperature. If you suspect diabetes you need to visit the vet.

Torpor

Torpor is a very deep sleep state like hibernation. Hamsters may sleep like this when the temperature falls. If your hamster's body is cool, and it's only breathing very, very softly, then your hamster may be in torpor.

To bring your hamster out of torpor, place a small blanket on them so that their body heat has a hard time escaping or move them to a warmer room than the one that they're currently in.

****
*   Sorry No Pics in This Section as too yucky to show   *
****

Training your hamster not to bite

Tame hamsters have been handled regularly, they are used to people and don't get scared easily. Hamsters that have not been handled much will not be very tame. They will bite if you try to pick them up because they're afraid. It's good to remember that biting is a response to fear not aggression.

Training a hamster requires a good deal of patience. It might take several weeks for your hamster to become accustomed to you. Here are a few simple steps that you can use to manage a hamster that bites.

Introduce Yourself

To start with you should introduce yourself to your hamster and allow them to get used to you. Spend time sat near the cage and talk to your hamster. Share your scent by placing a small item of clothing in the cage or keeping bedding in your hand for some time before adding it into the cage.

During this stage you may need to pick up your hamster to allow you to clean the habitat or clean the cage. You might want to use a towel or other soft cloth and scoop up your hamster.

Offer a Hand

Sitting next to the cage and talking to your hamster, offer a hand slowly inside the enclosure. Do not try to touch your hamster at this stage but them let explore your hand if they want to. Your hamster may choose just to sniff you or to walk across your fingers.

Offer Treats

Once your hamster is comfortable with your hand inside the cage, you can try to offer a treat.

Try to offer a treat and see if your hamster will take it from your fingers. Try again with the treat on you flat palm, does hammy climb on you to take the treat, pouch it and run off? If you are lucky, they may even sit in your palm to eat it.

Pet Your Hamster

Once your pet is taking treats, you can move on and try to pet your hamster. Try gently stroking their back with one or two fingers.

Pick Up Your Hamster

Now comes the moment that you have been waiting for. Time to pick up your hamster. Ready? Here are five golden rules to remember as you try.

Always Wash Hands Before Picking Up Your Hamster

Wash with an unscented soap. If you have been handling food or wash with fruit-scented soap, your hamster will smell your hand as food, guess what's coming?

Never Wake Your Hamster Suddenly From

In the wild, hamsters spend most of their time deep, deep underground, where they're rarely disturbed and they sleep deeply. If you try to wake your hamster suddenly with a hand, guess what's coming?

Never "Sneak Up"

When you are ready to pick up your hamster, let it see your hand first for a few seconds before you try to lift it. A sudden movement can be misinterpreted as an attack and your hamster will defend themselves.

Pick Up Your Hamster Carefully

When picking up your hamster always use two hands and put one hand under its bottom for support. Lift your hamster facing toward you rather than away from you as being picked up can be disorienting. Your hamster has some frame of reference looking at you and is less likely to jump.

Stay Calm

If your hamster looks ready to set its teeth on your fingers, pull your hand away slowly and smoothly so as not to frighten them more.

If hammy does close their teeth on your skin, the best way to make your hamster stop is to blow directly at their nose. Shouting, grabbing or any other kind of reaction will make your hamster more frightened, and bite harder.

Determine your hamster's sex

It's not hard to separate the boy hamsters from the girls once you know what to look for. You may have to wait a while though, until they are around a month old to be sure. Don't trust that the pet shop has sexed them properly, check for yourself.

Openings

Looking at the underside of your hamster, near the tail. There will be two openings, one of which is the anus (or bottom) and the other opening will be either the penis (boys) or the vulva (girls).

The most obvious difference between the two sexes is that boys have a bigger distance between the anus and penis, with a smallish but still obvious gap between them. Girls have only a very tiny space, between the vulva and anus, often so close together that they look like they are touching

Testicles

In male hamsters, testicles will develop and will become quite obvious as hammy gets older. When seen from underneath, they appear as noticeable swellings. As he matures, you can tell a hamster is male without turning him over as the testicles are large enough to give his rear end a pronounced pointed appearance.

The female's rear does not have these bulges, and looks smoother and more rounded. Remember that testicles are not obvious in very young hamsters, and the males also can retract them, so you may need to look closely at your hamster to be sure.

Nipples

Female hamsters will usually have two rows of nipples on their belly which can be seen if you run your finger gently along her underside, parting fur so that you can see down to her skin.

As with the boys' testicles, girls' nipples become more pronounced as they get older. If the girl has had babies, her nipples will be quite obvious and much easier to see.

A Boy

Made in United States
North Haven, CT
19 February 2023

32867889R00035